Homemade Meals in Minutes
Family-Friendly Menus Made Easy

Linda Spivey and Cinda Coon

Cloves   Cinnamon   Nutmeg

HARVEST HOUSE PUBLISHERS
EUGENE, OREGON

Homemade Meals in Minutes

Copyright © 2008 by Linda Spivey
Published by Harvest House Publishers
Eugene, OR 97402
www.harvesthousepublishers.com

ISBN-13: 978-0-7369-2200-5
ISBN-10: 0-7369-2200-8

Cover design and interior production by Garborg Design Works, Savage, Minnesota.

Printed in China
08 09 10 11 12 13 14 15 / RDS / 10 9 8 7 6 5 4 3 2 1

In our fast-paced world we try to fit more and more into our busy schedules.

We cut corners just to save a few minutes here and there. For many families, it's meal time that is cut out. Try to commit daily to a meal time together. Everyone has to eat, so share this time. Quality time together is the essential ingredient to keeping a family strong. And as you gather together, don't forget to take a moment to thank the Lord for the many blessings He has given.

I want to thank my sister Cinda Coon for her essential help in pulling together this collection of our favorite family recipes. Cinda loves to cook and make people happy with food. She is thrilled to just recently be opening her own restaurant in her town of Berkley, Michigan. I know the food will be great.

We hope you enjoy these recipes as much as our families do.

With love,
Linda and Cinda

Summer time Ahhh.....

KISS the cook

Salt   Seasoning   Pepper

4

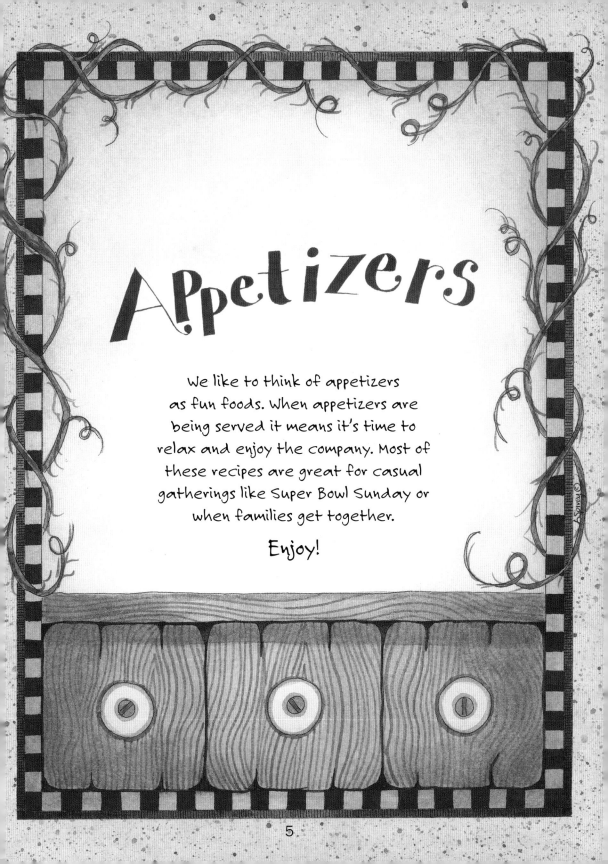

Appetizers

We like to think of appetizers
as fun foods. When appetizers are
being served it means it's time to
relax and enjoy the company. Most of
these recipes are great for casual
gatherings like Super Bowl Sunday or
when families get together.

Enjoy!

STROMBOLI

This hearty snack is great for a gathering like Super Bowl Sunday!

Dough:
   1 ½ cups milk
   1 ½ tablespoons olive oil
   ½ teaspoon sugar
   1 package dry yeast
   dash of salt
   3 cups flour or enough to
      make soft bread dough,
      kneaded lightly, not sticky.

Warm milk and add yeast to dissolve. Add other ingredients and let rise until dough doubles (1 ½ hours approx.). Punch down, place dough in a 10 x 15 x 1 greased cookie sheet with sides, spread to all the edges.

Spread almost to edges the following: a dab of melted butter, a layer of mustard, and Morton Nature's Seasons seasoning mix. Down the middle of the length layer the following:

¼-½ pound shaved ham
⅛-¼ pound chopped salami
⅛-¼ pound pepperoni
8 oz. grated mozzarella cheese
Place in thin layers, repeating once. Fold dough over lengthwise to the middle on both sides, then crimp together. Spread margarine on top and sprinkle with Nature's seasoning. Bake at 350 degrees for 35-40 minutes. Cut into 4-6 servings.

ALMOND NUT CHEESE BALL

This is an old family favorite.

   1 8-oz. package cream cheese
   ½ cup mayonnaise
   5 slices of crisp bacon
      crumbled
   1 tablespoon chopped
      green onion
   ½ teaspoon dill weed
   ⅛ teaspoon pepper
   1 ¼ cup sliced almonds to roll
      cheese ball in

Combine together cream cheese and mayonnaise, then add rest of ingredients and mix well. Shape into a ball and roll in nuts. Cover and chill overnight. Serve with crackers.

TACO DIP

This is a good dish for a gathering. Everyone loves it.

Cover a 10 x 15 x 1 cookie sheet with foil. Blend together in a bowl, then spread onto the cookie sheet:

  16 oz. sour cream
  1 large package of cream cheese
  1 can of bean dip

Sprinkle evenly on the sour cream layer:

  $\frac{1}{2}$ head shredded lettuce
  8 oz. taco sauce
  ripe olives, sliced
  3-4 tomatoes, chopped and drained
  1 medium sweet onion, chopped
  2 cups shredded cheddar cheese

Refrigerate several hours to set. Serve with tortilla chips.

GUACAMOLE DIP

You might want to make a double recipe. This will go fast!

  2 ripe avocados, skinned and mashed
  1 medium onion, chopped fine
  1 tablespoon lemon juice
  1 teaspoon salt
  coarse pepper
  1 tomato, chopped and peeled

Stir all together and serve with tortilla chips.

LINDA'S QUICK SALSA

My sister says this is "cheating," but it's a tasty shortcut that works.

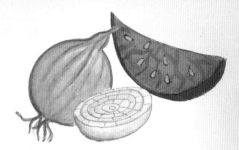

1 jar of your favorite salsa
2 fresh chopped tomatoes
½ sweet onion, chopped
Dash of garlic

Stir all together and serve with tortilla chips.

APPETIZER MEATBALLS

1 pound ground beef
½ cup bread crumbs
1 egg
⅔ cup milk
2 tablespoons finely
  chopped onion
1 teaspoon salt
⅛ teaspoon pepper
¼ teaspoon nutmeg
1 can mushrooms with juice

Mix all together, form into small meatballs. In a skillet, brown meatballs in a little oil, then remove fat. Add ½ cup water and mushrooms with juice. Simmer ½ hour, then serve.

VEGGIE PIZZA

A delicious munchie, great for a gathering.

Unroll 2 packages refrigerator crescent rolls, placing them on a 15 x 10 x 1 cookie sheet. Press all lines out to form the dough for the crust. Bake at 400 degrees for 10 minutes. Cool.

Mix together and spread on cooled crust:
2 8-oz. packages cream
  cheese, softened
⅔ cup mayonnaise
1 teaspoon dill weed
1 teaspoon garlic
1 teaspoon onion flakes

Top with your favorite vegetables: chopped cauliflower, green pepper, green onion, broccoli, mushrooms, carrots, etc. Chill, cut into squares.

Whatever you do, work at it with all your heart,
as working for the Lord.

Colossians 3:23

BACON & WATER CHESTNUT ROLL-UPS

A delicious appetizer!

1 pound bacon, cut in half
1 can whole water chestnuts

Roll each strip of bacon around one water chestnut, and hold together with a toothpick. Place on a plate with a paper towel. Cook in microwave on High for 6 minutes, then put on a foil-lined pan and pour sauce over.

Sauce — Mix together:
½ cup mayonnaise
½ cup brown sugar
½ cup chili sauce

Bake at 375 degrees for 30 minutes. If not cooked in the microwave first then bake for 1 hour. Serve warm.

CHILI CHEESE DIP

When you take this to a party make two recipes, because it goes fast.

1 8-oz. package cream cheese, softened
1 can (15 oz.) chili without beans
1 small can (4 oz.) chopped green chilies
8 oz. shredded cheddar or Colby Jack cheese

Spread cream cheese on the bottom of an 8 x 8 pan or pie pan, spread the green chilies over the cream cheese. Next, spread the chili, then top with cheese. Heat oven to 325 degrees and bake for 15 minutes...or heat in microwave for 5-6 minutes. Serve with tortilla chips.

CINDA'S FRESH GARDEN SALSA

Considerably more work, but worth the effort.

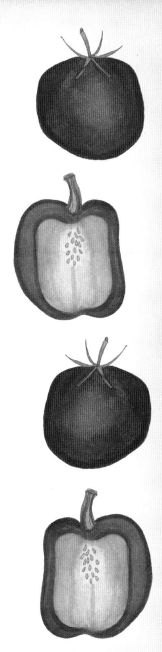

6-8 ripe tomatoes, scalded
  and peeled
1 yellow sweet pepper
1 whole jalapeno pepper,
  cored and seeded
  (see precautions below)*
1 bunch fresh cilantro—just
  the leaves, not the stems
juice of $\frac{1}{2}$ lemon
1 sweet onion or 1 bunch
  green onion
2-3 cloves of garlic
1 tablespoon sugar
1 small can of tomato paste
1-2 teaspoons kosher salt
dash of pepper

Finely chop all the ingredients, or place all but the tomatoes and the tomato sauce in a food processor and gently process. It should be chunky, not pureed. Add fresh tomatoes last and process gently again. Stir in the tomato paste. Serve with tortilla chips.

*Use caution when handling jalapeno peppers. Use gloves and avoid getting the juice on your skin.

Simple Pleasures
are
Life's Treasures

Rosemary   Bay Leaves   Thyme

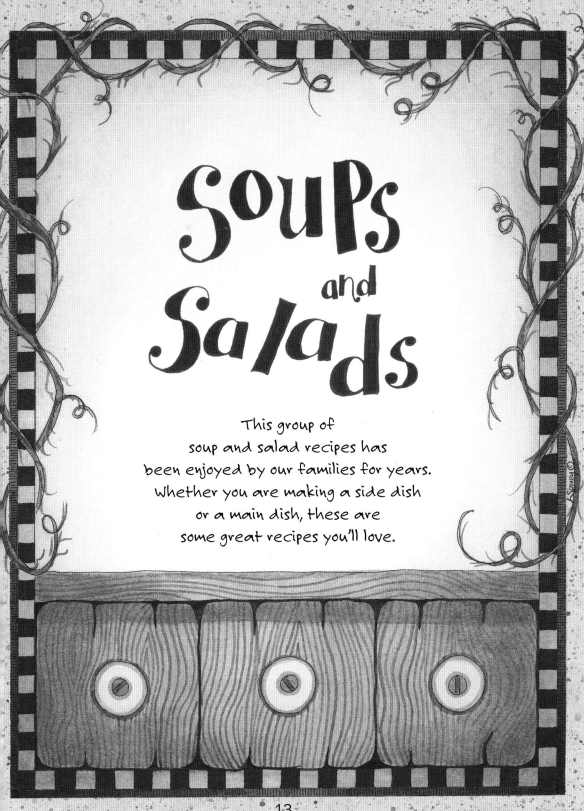

Soups and Salads

This group of
soup and salad recipes has
been enjoyed by our families for years.
Whether you are making a side dish
or a main dish, these are
some great recipes you'll love.

POTATO-CHEESE-BROCCOLI SOUP

This is an all-time family favorite, especially on a really chilly day.

6-7 potatoes
1 package onion soup mix
1 onion, chopped
milk
flour
1-2 cups cheddar cheese
  (save some to sprinkle on top)
broccoli, cut into small pieces

In a large soup kettle, place peeled potatoes cut into ½-inch pieces. Cover halfway with water. Add onion soup mix and chopped onion. Simmer 15-20 minutes, or until potatoes are tender but firm. Add 1 cup of milk for each serving. For each cup of milk used, add 1½ tablespoons flour to thicken. To blend flour, place flour and some milk in a cup or jar with a lid and shake to mix. Pour into kettle of potatoes and stir. Bring to a boil, stirring constantly. Lower heat and stir in shredded cheddar cheese. Add broccoli pieces. Stir and simmer until broccoli is tender. Serve piping hot with cheese sprinkled on top.

LINDA'S POTATO SALAD

After years of trial and error, I finally perfected my recipe. Hope you like it too.

7-8 potatoes
6-7 eggs, hard boiled

Peel potatoes and cut into ½-inch pieces. Place in a pan with 2 inches of water and bring to a boil. Lower heat and simmer for 15-20 minutes, just until tender but still firm in shape. While this is cooking, hard-boil eggs. Place eggs in a saucepan, cover with cold water. Bring to a boil, cover and reduce heat to low. Cook 30 minutes. Remove from heat and run under cold water. Older eggs will peel easier than very fresh eggs.

In a large bowl mix together approx.:
  ½–¾ cup mayonnaise
  1 medium sweet onion, chopped
  ½–¾ cup sweet relish
  a generous amount of mustard
    (perhaps 1-2 tablespoons
    or more)
  salt to taste

Add cooked (but cooled) potatoes to the mayonnaise mixture. When this is well blended, gently stir in cut up hard-boiled eggs. Place in a serving bowl, and smooth out the top. Place egg slices and a sprinkle of paprika on top to decorate it. Refrigerate until cold before serving.

CHUNKY TOMATO SOUP

This soup is delicious, quick, and easy.

In a large saucepan sauté 1 medium onion in 1 tablespoon butter. Add:

    2 cans tomato soup
    2 cans (14 oz.) diced tomatoes including liquid
    1 ½ cups milk
    1-3 teaspoons sugar
    ½-1 teaspoon basil
    ½ teaspoon garlic

Bring to a boil, then reduce heat and simmer 10-15 minutes.

VEGETARIAN VEGETABLE SOUP

We love to make a big kettle of this, enough to last several days.

In a large soup kettle combine:

    1 large can of tomato juice
    1 can of water
    6-8 bouillon cubes
    ½ head of cabbage, shredded
    1 large onion, chopped
    2 cups frozen French-style green beans
    2 cups frozen cauliflower
    salt to taste
    sweeten to taste

Simmer covered for one hour. The last 15 minutes of cooking time add ½ to 1 cup alphabet noodles or small noodles.

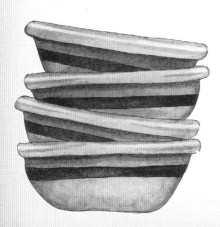

TACO SALAD

This is a great summertime meal, when sweet onions and tomatoes are in season.

1 pound hamburger
1-2 teaspoons cumin powder
  or to taste
salt to taste
1 head of lettuce, torn
4 tomatoes, chopped
ripe olives, cut into slices
1 large sweet onion, chopped
1-2 cups grated cheddar
  cheese
salsa
sour cream
tortilla chips

Cook the hamburger until done, removing excess fat. Stir cumin powder and salt into the crumbly hamburger. Cool.

Make individual salads with a generous bottom layer of lettuce sprinkled with chopped onion pieces. Add hearty spoonfuls of the seasoned hamburger to the top of the lettuce. Sprinkle on the cheese, tomato pieces, and olive slices. Just before eating add the tortilla chips around the edge of the salad. Top with sour cream and salsa. This is a complete meal.

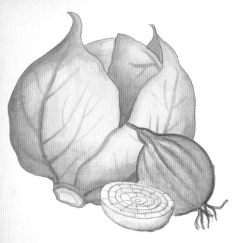

VEGETABLE BEEF SOUP

A hearty meal, almost like a stew.

In a large soup kettle, place a 1-2 pound beef roast, covered with water. Add 2 medium-sized chopped onions. Simmer several hours until meat falls apart easily. After the meat is cooked, shred the meat, remove the fat off the top of the broth and add: 1 large can of tomatoes and the liquid. Cut up tomatoes. Add your choice of chopped vegetables, such as carrots, potatoes, celery, and cabbage. Simmer all the vegetables until tender. Salt, pepper, and sweeten to taste.

CHINESE NOODLE SALAD

This salad is so delicious, we think it's "addicting." Once you start eating it, you can't stop.

    romaine lettuce, torn into
        small pieces
    1 bunch green onions,
        chopped
    add other lettuce of your
        choice (optional)

Sauté and cool:
    4 oz. sliced almonds
    1 stick butter
    2 packages ramen noodles,
        broken up, without the
        seasoning
    1 oz. sesame seeds

Boil and cool:
    ¾ cup salad oil
    ½ cup sugar
    ¼ cup cider vinegar
    1 teaspoon soy sauce

Make sure everything is cool before tossing all together...toss together just before serving.

SPINACH SALAD

The perfect summer salad.

Dressing:
Mix together in a jar:
    ½ cup sugar
    1 cup oil
    ⅓ cup vinegar
    ⅓ cup catsup
    1 tablespoon
    Worcestershire sauce

Salad:
    1 bag spinach 16 oz.
    1 8-oz. can sliced
        water chestnuts
    3 strips bacon, cooked
        and crumbled
    handful of fresh bean sprouts
    sliced red onion
    3 hard-boiled eggs, chopped
    grated Colby or cheddar
        cheese

Mix with salad dressing and serve.

Welcome

Bless us, O Lord,
for these Thy gifts, which
we are about to receive
from Thy bounty, through
Christ our Lord. Amen.

RASPBERRY GELATIN

Bottom layer:
Combine ingredients. Pour into 9 x 13 pan or gelatin mold and let set.
- 1 small package raspberry gelatin
- 1 cup boiling water
- 1 10-oz. package frozen raspberries

Top layer:
- 1 package unflavored gelatin
- ½ cup cold water

Dissolve these together, then stir in 1 cup sugar and 1 cup of half-and-half cream.

Heat in a double boiler for 10 minutes, stirring constantly until it boils. Let cool. Stir in 1 cup sour cream. Pour over the bottom layer. Refrigerate to set.

3-LAYER GELATIN SALAD

A favorite at our house. Fancy enough for a holiday gathering.

1st layer: Mix and place in a serving bowl:
- 1 4-oz. package cherry gelatin
- 1 4-oz. package raspberry gelatin
- 2 cups boiling water

Dissolve gelatin, then add 1 can (16 oz.) crushed pineapple, drained. Refrigerate until set.

2nd layer: Cook 1 small package vanilla pudding mix, cool. Spoon on top of the set pineapple/gelatin, until smooth. Refrigerate to set.

3rd layer: Using a mixer, mix together 1 prepared package of Dream Whip or about 1 cup of Cool Whip with 1 large package (8 oz.) of cream cheese, softened. Smooth on top of the pudding layer. Allow to set overnight or at least a few hours.

ANGEL HAIR PASTA SALAD

1 pound of angel hair pasta
4 large cucumbers
1 package fresh dill, chopped
2 packages ranch
  dressing mix
salt

Break the pasta in half and cook according to the directions. Drain and cool.

Peel and finely grate the cucumbers and place in a colander. Sprinkle with salt and let set for 10-15 minutes. Press the excess water out of the cucumbers. (I use my salad spinner to remove the excess water.)

Mix the ranch dressing according to the directions. Add the chopped dill and the cucumbers, and blend together.

Blend into the cooked pasta. Allow to chill in the refrigerator several hours to meld flavors before serving.

SWEET BROCCOLI SALAD

1 bunch of broccoli cut into
  small pieces
1 small sweet onion, chopped
½ cup raisins
1 ½ cups sunflower seeds

Dressing:
1 cup mayonnaise
⅓ cup sugar
¼ cup vinegar

Mix the dressing with the broccoli mix. Refrigerate 1 hour to marinate the flavors.

We love chicken salad. Here are three great versions.

CHICKEN SALAD SUPREME

Add to 2 cups cooked, cubed chicken:
  mayonnaise
  seedless grapes, cut in half

Stir together and place on a bed of lettuce. Sprinkle cashews on top and serve with croissants.

LINDA'S FAVORITE CHICKEN SALAD

2 cups cooked, cubed chicken
  $\frac{1}{2}$ sweet onion chopped
  $\frac{1}{2}$ cup chopped pecans
  mayonnaise
  salt to taste

Stir all together with enough mayo to make it creamy. Place on a bed of lettuce. Sprinkle with more chopped pecans. Serve with a croissant roll.

CINDY'S CHICKEN SALAD

  1 pound boneless, skinless
    chicken breast cooked
    and cubed
  3 stalks celery, chopped
  1 $\frac{1}{2}$ teaspoons fresh or
    dried dill weed
  1 teaspoon salt
  $\frac{1}{4}$ teaspoon pepper
  mayonnaise

Mix together, adding enough mayonnaise to make it creamy. Let sit 1 hour to let flavors blend.

24-HOUR FRUIT SALAD

This luscious salad has been a part of our holiday meals since we were children.

Drain all fruit and set aside:
  2 ½ cups pineapple tidbits (reserve 2 tablespoons pineapple juice)
  2 cups pitted Royal Ann cherries
  2-3 oranges, pared, cut into pieces

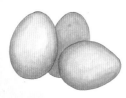

Custard:
Place the 2 tablespoons reserved pineapple juice in a small double boiler and add:
  3 egg yolks, beaten
  2 tablespoons sugar
  2 tablespoons vinegar
  dash of salt
  1 tablespoon butter

Cook custard until thick and lightly coats the spoon. Stir into the fruit.

Whip 1 cup of whipping cream until stiff. Combine whipped cream with 1 cup of mini-marshmallows. Add the fruit/custard mixture, stirring to mix completely. Pour into a serving bowl, cover and chill 24 hours before serving.

By wisdom a house is built,
and through understanding it is established;
Through knowledge its rooms are filled
with rare and beautiful treasures.

Proverbs 24:3-4

Give Us This Day
Our Daily Bread

Salt Baking Powder Soda

Bread,
Muffins, and Rolls

These tried and true recipes help to make any meal complete. Our very favorite is the Butterhorn Rolls. We don't have a holiday meal without them.

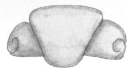

BUTTERHORN ROLLS

We adapted an old family recipe to use with a bread machine. We use the bread machine to mix, knead, and do the first rise. Then we shape the dough into the rolls for that home baked look.

¾ cup milk, heat to scalding (just before boiling)

To the hot milk add:
½ cup shortening
½ cup sugar
2 teaspoons salt
3 beaten eggs

Pour this mixture into bread machine pan. Add 4 ⅓ cups flour. Sprinkle 1 package of yeast (or 2 ½ teaspoons bread machine yeast) on top of flour. Set machine to just mix and knead dough. After the dough has mixed, kneaded, and risen once, remove from machine. Roll out half of the dough into a large circle, approx. 12 inches. Brush with melted butter. Cut into pie-shaped wedges and roll up beginning at the wide end. Place on a baking sheet, tucking the point under. Brush with melted butter. Allow to rise until double. Bake at 400 degrees for 10-12 minutes or until golden brown.

MONKEY BREAD

You'll go bananas for this one. Great for a breakfast treat.

3 packages of refrigerator biscuits

Cut each biscuit into fourths. Melt 1 stick butter in pan, adding the cut biscuits. Sprinkle in 2 tablespoons cinnamon and 1 ½ cups sugar. Mix all together and put evenly into a bundt pan. Bake at 350 degrees for ½ hour, until golden brown. Turn out onto a plate. Serve warm.

RAISIN BRAN MUFFINS

An all-time favorite.

1 ¼ cups flour
1 tablespoon baking powder
½ teaspoon salt
½ cup sugar
1 egg, beaten
¼ cup vegetable oil
1 teaspoon cinnamon
2 ½ cups raisin bran cereal
1 ¼ cups milk

Combine the cereal and milk, allow to sit for 5 minutes. Then add the rest of the ingredients, stirring well. Pour into muffin tins, lined with paper muffin cups. Bake at 400 degrees for 20 minutes, or until golden brown. Serve hot.

GARLIC CHEESE BREADSTICKS

A real favorite with spaghetti or lasagna.

½ cup butter
2 ½ cups flour
4 teaspoons baking powder
1 ⅓ cups milk
2 teaspoons garlic powder
Parmesan cheese

Melt butter in a 9 x 13 pan. In a bowl mix the flour, baking powder, and milk, stirring until dough is formed. Knead about 3 minutes, adding extra flour if needed so it's not sticky. Roll into 8-inch squares, cut in half, then into 4-inch strips. Dip both sides in butter and sprinkle with garlic powder and Parmesan cheese. Bake at 450 degrees for 15-20 minutes.

CORN BREAD

If you like a sweeter corn bread, then this one's for you.

$\frac{1}{4}$ cup vegetable oil
1 cup yellow cornmeal
1 cup flour
$\frac{1}{3}$ cup sugar
1 tablespoon baking powder
$\frac{1}{2}$ teaspoon salt
1 cup milk
2 eggs, beaten

Combine all the ingredients in a bowl until smooth. Pour into a greased 9 x 9 pan.

Bake at 425 degrees for 20-25 minutes until golden brown. Serve hot.

ZUCCHINI BREAD

3 eggs
2 teaspoons vanilla
1 cup vegetable oil
2 cups sugar
3 cups flour
2 cups zucchini, peeled, grated, firmly packed
2 teaspoons baking powder
1 teaspoon salt
3 teaspoons cinnamon
1 teaspoon baking soda
1 cup chopped walnuts

Combine all ingredients, mixing well. Pour into two greased and floured loaf pans. Bake at 325 degrees for 1 hour.

BLUEBERRY MUFFINS

A delicious addition to any meal.

½ cup butter
2 cups flour
2 eggs
½ teaspoon salt
2 teaspoons baking powder
1 ¼ cups sugar
½ cup milk
2 ½ cups blueberries

Cream together the butter and sugar, add eggs, and mix well. Add dry ingredients, alternating with the milk. Mash ½ cup blueberries and stir in by hand. Stir in remaining berries. Pour into greased muffin tins, or use paper liners. Fill half full. Sprinkle with sugar. Bake at 375 degrees for 25 to 30 minutes.
Makes 22-24 muffins.

PUMPKIN BREAD

This makes 3 loaves, enough to give a gift to a neighbor or friend.

4 eggs
2 cups brown sugar
2 cups granulated sugar
1 large can of pumpkin
1 cup vegetable oil
5 cups flour
4 teaspoons baking soda
1 teaspoon salt
1 tablespoon ground cloves
1 tablespoon ground cinnamon
1 cup chopped walnuts

Mix all the ingredients together. Pour into 3 greased loaf pans, half full. Bake at 350 degrees for 1 hour. Cool on a rack.

ANNA LEE'S COFFEE CAKE

This is quick to make and delicious enough to keep you going back for more.

2 cups flour
2 cups brown sugar
1 teaspoon baking powder
¼ teaspoon salt
1-2 teaspoons cinnamon
½ cup butter
1 cup buttermilk
1 teaspoon baking soda
1 egg

Combine the first five dry ingredients and cut in the butter until evenly crumbly. Set aside 1 cup crumbs for the topping. Add the baking soda to the buttermilk and mix with the egg. Pour into the dry ingredient mixture and mix well. Pour into a 9 x 13 cake pan, and sprinkle the reserved crumbs on top. Bake at 375 degrees for 20 minutes, or until golden brown. Serve warm.

If you don't have buttermilk on hand try this: In a measuring cup place 2 tablespoons vinegar and add enough milk to make one cup. Allow to sit a few minutes to thicken.

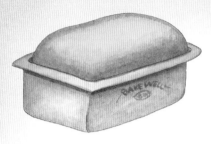

BANANA BREAD

This delicious bread makes one loaf.

½ cup vegetable oil
1 cup sugar
1 teaspoon baking soda
2 eggs, beaten
3 very ripe bananas, mashed
2 cups flour
½ cup walnuts

Mix all the ingredients together and pour into a greased and floured loaf pan. Bake at 325 degrees for 1 hour.

Our Daily Bread

HOMEMADE BISCUITS

Do you like flaky biscuits? Here's the secret.

In a mixing bowl blend together:
- 2 cups flour
- 3 teaspoons baking powder
- 1 teaspoon salt
- 1 tablespoon sugar

Cut in ⅓ cup soft shortening.

Quickly stir in ¾ cup milk, stirring only about ½ minute. Turn out onto a floured surface and lightly knead about ½ minute. Minimal handling makes for flakier biscuits. Cut out with a biscuit cutter, being careful not to twist. Place on a cookie sheet and bake at 450 degrees for 12-15 minutes or until lightly golden brown.

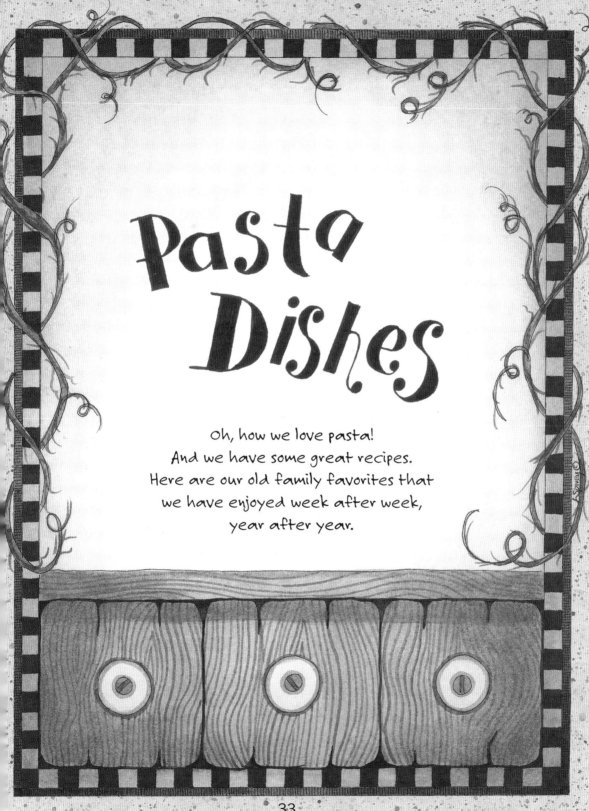

Pasta Dishes

Oh, how we love pasta!
And we have some great recipes.
Here are our old family favorites that
we have enjoyed week after week,
year after year.

ITALIAN SPAGHETTI SAUCE

This is a true Italian recipe. It was Grandpa Jacobucci's, who came to America from Italy. The original recipe instructed to allow it to "blump," which we interpret as "simmer."

2 small cans tomato paste
1 large can whole tomatoes
8 small cans of water
   (use the tomato paste cans)
1-2 cloves of fresh
   garlic, chopped
2-3 bay leaves
oregano to cover top
parsley to cover top
salt and pepper
Parmesan cheese to cover top

Combine all ingredients in a large saucepan and heat to a boil. Add Italian Meatballs. Reduce heat to medium and simmer (blump). Cook without a lid for 4 hours to blend all the spices. Serve over fresh cooked pasta.

ITALIAN MEATBALLS
Meatballs for the spaghetti sauce

1 pound ground beef
1 egg
1 clove fresh garlic, finely
   chopped
1 teaspoon parsley flakes
1 teaspoon oregano
salt and pepper
a couple of shakes of
   Parmesan cheese
1 slice of bread ripped into
   tiny pieces

Mix all together and form into small meatballs. Brown in a little oil, then add to spaghetti sauce.

PERFECT PASTA

For perfect pasta, bring water to a boil and maintain the water boiling for the entire cooking time. Cook until tender. We always add a tablespoon of olive oil to the water. It helps to keep the noodles from sticking together. Serve immediately.

MOM'S SPAGHETTI SAUCE

This is our mother's recipe, and a family favorite. We remember her cooking it and adding all the herbs, saying it was a "secret recipe." Mom says it's all right to share it with you now. We hope you like it as much as we do.

Brown hamburger and onion together until completely cooked, remove fat. Stir all the other ingredients together, and add water to make the right consistency. Simmer on low heat for ½-1 hour. Serve on fresh cooked pasta. Sprinkle on Parmesan cheese.

1 pound hamburger
1 large onion, chopped
1 large can tomato sauce (28 oz.)
1 small can tomato paste (8 oz.)
1 tablespoon basil
1 tablespoon oregano
1 teaspoon garlic
1-2 tablespoons sugar to taste
salt to taste

Add more or less of above spices to taste.

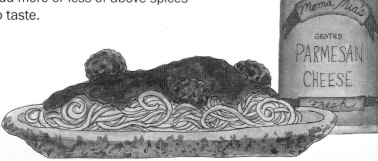

BEEF-NOODLE CASEROLE

A hearty meal, quick to fix.

1 pound of hamburger
1 large onion, chopped
1 ½ cups dry
   macaroni noodles
1 can of tomato soup
sugar to taste
salt and pepper
sprinkle of garlic
2 tomatoes cut-up or a small
   can of tomatoes
2 cup grated cheddar cheese

Brown hamburger and onion in a skillet and remove fat. Cook (in another pan) the macaroni noodles until tender. Stir the tomato soup into the cooked hamburger, add the drained noodles. Add salt and pepper and garlic to taste. Sprinkle in a teaspoon (more or less) of sugar. Add the tomatoes and the cheese. Reserve enough cheese to sprinkle on top. Simmer until hot. If you are in a hurry you can serve it just like this. If you have more time, pour into a casserole bowl, sprinkle with cheese and bake in a 350 degree oven until golden brown.

FETTUCINE ALFREDO

This is a quick and easy meal that is sure to please.

1 pound cooked fettuccine noodles

In a saucepan over medium heat, combine:
   ½ stick of butter with
    2 tablespoons flour
Slowly stir in:
1 cup milk
½ cup of sour cream
1 cup Parmesan cheese
1 teaspoon fresh parsley
garlic to taste

Bring to a low boil, then toss with cooked fettuccine noodles. This is good just as it is, or you could add cooked chicken or shrimp and/or cooked broccoli to the sauce.

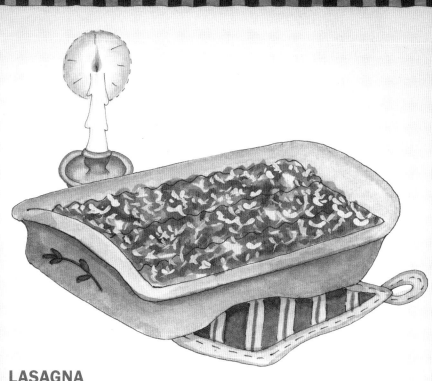

LASAGNA

Use "Mom's Spaghetti Sauce."

lasagna noodles
ricotta cheese
mozzarella cheese

Make spaghetti sauce, and cook lasagna noodles until tender, drain. Layer in a baking pan the noodles, sauce, ricotta cheese, and mozzarella. The average-sized cake pan will hold 3 lasagna noodles wide with 3 layers. Top it with sauce and sprinkle with mozzarella cheese.

Be sure to completely cover the top layer of the noodles with sauce and cheese. Otherwise the noodles will dry out in the oven. Bake at 350 degrees for about 45 minutes or until the top starts to turn a golden brown. This could be prepared ahead of time, then kept in the refrigerator until you are ready to bake it. If putting it in the oven totally cold, it will take longer to bake, about 1-1 ½ hours. Serve with a salad and garlic bread.

I will praise you, O Lord, with all my heart;
I will tell of all your wonders. Psalm 9:1

HAMBURGER STROGANOFF

1 pound hamburger
1 small onion, chopped
1 can mushroom soup
½ cup or more sour cream
Worcestershire sauce
sprinkle of garlic
sliced fresh mushrooms
2-3 cups noodles

Brown hamburger with the chopped onion, remove the fat. Add the mushroom soup and ½ cup (more or less) of sour cream. Add fresh mushrooms. Sprinkle in some garlic and a teaspoon or two of Worcestershire sauce. Simmer on low heat until hot. Serve over hot cooked noodles.

CHICKEN-MACARONI BAKE

2 cups cooked macaroni
2 cups diced cooked chicken
2 cans mushroom soup
1 cup milk
½ pound cheddar cheese
herb bread crumbs for the top

Combine all the ingredients and pour into a 9 x 13 pan. Sprinkle top with the bread crumbs. Bake at 350 degrees for 45-60 minutes.

SAVORY CHICKEN NOODLE CASSEROLE

12-oz. package of noodles
1 can cream of chicken soup
2 cups milk
½ cup grated Parmesan
  cheese
3 cups diced, cooked chicken
2 cups chopped broccoli
½ cup chopped celery
½ teaspoon poultry seasoning
salt to taste

Cook pasta according to package directions, drain. Stir together with the remaining ingredients. Pour into a 3-quart casserole dish. Cover and bake at 350 degrees for 40-60 minutes until hot and bubbly.

Suppertime Brings Us Together

Sage   Thyme   Basil

Hearty Dishes

Some of our recipes are very basic,
but we love them! Perhaps you have
your family's version of these.
Let's compare.

BREADED TURKEY CUTLETS

This is a family favorite. The important part is that the meat is cut thinner, and is boneless. We always try to make extras because they make a good lunch the next day.

4-6 turkey breast cutlets,
  $\frac{1}{4}$ to $\frac{1}{2}$ inch thick
1-2 eggs, whipped with a fork
$\frac{1}{2}$ cup flour
sprinkle of salt
1-2 cups cracker crumbs
oil to pan fry

Dip the cutlets first in the flour/salt mixture, then dip into the beaten egg, then into the cracker crumbs until well covered. Place in a heated skillet with about $\frac{1}{4}$ inch of cooking oil, and pan fry until golden brown on both sides. Place on a paper towel to absorb excess oil.

GRANDMA'S CREAMED CHICKEN

6 tablespoons butter
6 tablespoons flour
1 teaspoon salt
$\frac{1}{8}$ teaspoon pepper

In a large saucepan, melt butter and blend in flour. Remove from heat and slowly stir in:

1 $\frac{1}{2}$ cup seasoned chicken
  broth
1 cup cream

Bring to a boil, stirring constantly. Boil 1 minute.

Gently stir in:

1 cup cooked chicken
$\frac{1}{2}$ cup chopped green pepper
1 small can mushrooms,
  drained

Serve over Homemade Biscuits.

CHICKEN AND RICE

Our families love this classic meal.

    2-4 chicken breasts,
      boneless/with skin
    1 can mushroom soup
    1 cup regular white rice

In a flat skillet, brown 2-4 chicken breasts with a little oil until golden brown. After browning, remove chicken pieces and pour off fat. Add in 1 can cream of mushroom soup, slowly stir in 2 cups water. Do this slowly so you won't have lumps. Stir in 1 cup of regular rice, then place chicken pieces on top of the uncooked rice. Cook on medium-low heat for 1 hour.

BAKED CHICKEN

This is a regular favorite at our house, simple to fix but always delicious.

    raw, cut-up bone-in chicken
      with skin
    garlic powder
    salt

Line a broiler pan or cookie sheet with aluminum foil. Place chicken pieces evenly, not too crowded, and skin side up. Sprinkle with salt and garlic powder. Bake at 375 degrees for 1 hour.

Happiness....
is meant
to be Shared.

Sugar C...
2 cups sug...
1 cup butt...
2 egg...
2 tea. vanil...
2 tea. bakin...
1 Tab. vine...
½ cup mi...

Cloves   Cinnamon   Nutmeg

HAMBURGER PASTRIES

These take a bit more time to make, but are worth the effort.

Special pastry:
    1 cup flour
    ½ cup butter, softened
    3 oz. cream cheese, softened
    ½ teaspoon poppy seeds

Mix all the ingredients until well blended. Chill if possible. Roll thin and cut into 12 4-inch squares.

Meat filling:
    1 pound hamburger
    1 onion, minced
    1 teaspoon salt
    dash of pepper
    1 teaspoon Worcestershire
        sauce
    1 tablespoon tomato paste
    ¼ cup sour cream

Brown the hamburger and onion together until cooked, remove fat. Set aside ½ cup of the cooked hamburger/onion combination for the gravy. Remove from heat and add the rest of the ingredients, stirring to mix. Place about 3 tablespoons meat mixture in the center of the rolled out pastry squares. Top with another pastry square, crimp edges with a fork. Prick with a fork. Bake on a cookie sheet at 400 degrees for 15-20 minutes, or until lightly browned. Serve with Country Gravy.

COUNTRY GRAVY

In a saucepan combine the reserved hamburger/onion mixture and 3 tablespoons flour. Slowly add 1 ½ cups milk, stirring and cooking on medium heat until it comes to a boil and is thick. Salt and pepper to taste.

Rejoice always, pray without ceasing,
in everything give thanks.

1 Thessalonians 5:16-18

LINDA'S EASY SLOPPY JOE SANDWICHES

An all-time family favorite, kids love it.

1 pound hamburger
1 medium onion, chopped
barbecue sauce/catsup
1-2 tablespoons rolled oats
buns

Brown the hamburger and onion, remove fat. Stir in a mixture of half barbecue sauce and half catsup until it's the right consistency. If you want a spicier Sloppy Joe use more barbecue sauce, less spicy use more catsup. Add the oats to thicken. Simmer on low until hot. Serve on buns. This also makes a good Coney Dog, served with hot dogs on hot dog buns. Don't forget the mustard and relish.

CINDA'S SLOPPY JOES

A little sibling rivalry here... which one do you like best?

1 pound ground beef
¼ cup green pepper, chopped
¼ cup celery, chopped
½ cup onion, chopped
1 small can tomato sauce
¼ cup catsup
1 tablespoon vinegar
1 tablespoon brown sugar
1 teaspoon Worcestershire
    sauce
1 teaspoon salt

Brown ground beef, drain fat. Add all ingredients and simmer for 20 minutes. Serve on buns.

CHICKEN AND DUMPLINGS

In a large pot or Dutch oven, place a whole chicken. Cover with water. Add 2-3 celery stalks, 2-3 cut up carrots, 1 small cut up onion, and a sprinkle of parsley. Bring to a boil, then lower heat and simmer 1 ½ to 2 hours, or until tender. Remove chicken from the pan, debone meat, and set aside.

To prepare the chicken broth for the dumplings, I like to pour the broth through a strainer for a smoother texture. I also remove the fat from the top.

DUMPLINGS

3 cups flour
6 teaspoons baking powder
1 ½ teaspoons salt
1 ½ cups milk
6 tablespoons salad oil

Prepare the dumplings while the chicken is cooking. Stir dumpling ingredients together, then pour onto a floured surface. Knead in extra flour until it is not sticky. Roll out to a thickness of about ¼ inch to ½ inch. Sprinkle extra flour on the dumplings. Cut into 1 inch squares. Drop into boiling chicken broth, stirring occasionally. Broth will thicken with the extra flour sprinkled on the dumplings. Simmer 20-25 minutes. Serve with the chicken.

WELCOME

Let them give thanks to the
Lord...for he satisfies the
thirsty and fills the hungry
with good things.

Psalm 107:8-9

Earl Gray   Herbal   Orange Spice

PORCUPINE MEATBALLS

The name of this one will grab your attention. After you see it cooked you will understand why it has this name.

Lightly grease a 2 ½ qt. casserole that has a tight-fitting cover. Prepare in a saucepan and set aside the "Quick Tomato Sauce."

QUICK TOMATO SAUCE

Sauté in 2 tablespoons butter until tender:
    1 small onion, chopped
    ⅓ cup celery, chopped
    ⅓ cup green pepper, chopped

Add:
    1 can of tomato soup (10 oz.)
    1 cup water
    2 teaspoons lemon juice
    1-2 teaspoons
      Worcestershire sauce
    2 tablespoons brown sugar
    1 teaspoon dry mustard
    salt and pepper to taste

Prepare the meatballs, shape into 1 ½ inch balls:
    1 pound ground beef
    ½ cup uncooked regular rice
    ¼ cup minced onion
    1 teaspoon salt
    dash of pepper

Place meatballs into the casserole bowl, pour over the meatballs the "Quick Tomato Sauce." Cover and bake for 1 hour at 350 degrees, or until rice is tender.

FAVORITE MEATLOAF

2 pounds hamburger
½ cup onion, chopped fine
1 cup bread or cracker crumbs
1 tablespoon horseradish
1 teaspoon dry mustard
1 teaspoon salt
dash of pepper
2 eggs
¼ cup milk

Mix together in a bowl, everything but the hamburger. After this is done, add the hamburger and blend together well. Place in a loaf pan and bake at 350 degrees for 1 to 1 ½ hours until well browned. After it is completely baked, remove the fat. Cover with Tomato Sauce Glaze. Place back in oven a few minutes to heat glaze.

TOMATO SAUCE GLAZE

½ cup catsup
¼ brown sugar (or to taste)

Stir together and pour over the cooked meatloaf.

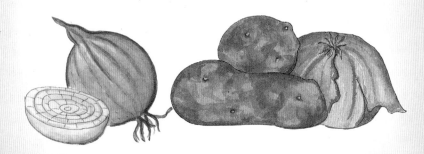

STUFFED PEPPER CUPS

6 medium green peppers
1 pound ground beef
⅓ cup onion, chopped
1 16-oz. can tomatoes, cut up
½ cup uncooked rice
1 teaspoon Worcestershire
  sauce
4 oz. sharp cheddar
  cheese, grated

Cut off the tops of the peppers and remove seeds and membranes. Precook peppers in boiling salt water for 5 minutes, drain (for crisp peppers omit pre-cooking). Sprinkle inside of peppers generously with salt. Brown meat with onions. Remove fat. Add ½ teaspoon salt and dash of pepper. Stir in tomatoes, rice, ½ cup of water and Worcestershire sauce. Cover, simmer 15 minutes until rice is tender. Stir in cheese.

Stuff peppers with the rice/meat combination and place in baking dish. Sprinkle grated cheese on top. Bake at 350 degrees for 20-25 minutes. Serves 6. This freezes very well.

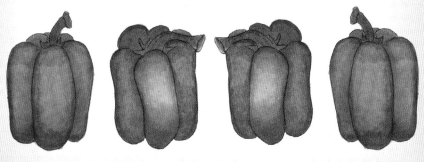

CABBAGE ROLLS/ GOLOMKI

This was our Grandma's recipe. She called these cabbage rolls Golomki.

  1 large head of cabbage
  ½ cup regular rice
  1 large onion, chopped fine
  ¾ pound ground beef
  ¼ pound ground pork (or use
    1 pound of ground beef)
  1 tablespoon bacon drippings
  salt and pepper
  1 egg

Tomato sauce to top the Golomki:
  1 can (1 pound) of tomato
    paste
  ½ cup water
  sugar to taste

Fill a large kettle ⅔ full with water, bring to a boil. Place whole cabbage head in the boiling water and simmer gently about 5 minutes or until leaves are soft yet crisp. Remove the cooked outer leaves, leaving the cabbage head in the water to cook the next layer of leaves. Remove each layer of leaves as they become soft. Cool the cooked leaves in cold water and set aside. In a large skillet, cook the ground beef, pork, and onion until cooked thoroughly. Remove fat. Add rice, 1 tablespoon of bacon drippings (a similar flavor can be achieved with sprinkling in Old Hickory Smoked Salt if you don't want to use the fat). Add 1 cup of water and seasoning. Simmer 15-20 minutes until rice is tender. After this mixture is cooked, and while it is still very hot, add one egg and stir very well. Place spoonfuls of the mixture into the whole cabbage leaves. Fold the sides inward and roll up. Place into a baking dish. Pour the Tomato Sauce over the cabbage rolls, bake uncovered at 350 degrees for 1 hour.

May the LORD, the Maker of heaven and earth, bless you.

Psalm 134:3

NEVER ENOUGH THYME

Rose Petal Potpourri

Spearmint   Lavender   Peppermint

DELICIOUS GRILLED PORK CHOPS

Marinate for a half hour, ½-inch cut pork chops in an oil type Italian salad dressing.

Cook on a hot grill, turning once.

While grilling, occasionally dip chops in:
¼ cup barbecue sauce
¼ cup Italian salad dressing
1-2 teaspoons sugar

GRANDMA'S SALMON PATTIES

1 large can salmon, remove the skin and bones
1 egg
½ cup cornmeal
¼ cup flour
1 medium onion, diced
dash of salt and pepper

Mix all together and shape into patties. Pan fry in vegetable oil until well browned on both sides.

WHITE CHICKEN CHILI

This is a mild chili, and it cooks up quick.

2 cups cooked chicken, cut up
4 cups chicken broth
1 - 2 cans Northern white
   beans
1 large onion, chopped
sprinkle of garlic powder
2-4 teaspoons cumin
1 4-oz can green chilies
2 tablespoons cornstarch
Monterey Jack cheese, grated

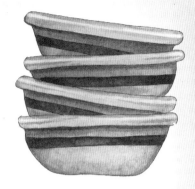

In a soup kettle:
Saute onion in a little oil. Stir cornstarch into cold broth and add to the onions. Stir in all the other ingredients and bring to a boil. Simmer 15 minutes. Serve topped with the cheese.

CHILI

1 pound hamburger
1 large onion, chopped
1 can tomato soup
1 large can tomato sauce
1 16-oz. can of kidney beans
1 16-oz. jar of salsa
1-2 tablespoons sugar or to taste
salt to taste
2-3 teaspoons cumin
1 teaspoon chili powder

Brown hamburger with the onion in a large kettle. Stir all the ingredients together and simmer for ½ -1 hour. Add water if too thick. Serve with grated cheddar cheese sprinkles on top.

GRANDMA'S COUNTRY PORK CHOPS

Grandma would make these when company came.

Small, thin-cut pork chops. First wash off chops with water, getting them wet. Then dip chops in a mixture of:

$\frac{1}{2}$ cup flour
$\frac{1}{2}$ cup cornmeal
dash of salt and pepper

Once chops are well coated, pan fry in a hot skillet using vegetable oil. Cook until well browned on both sides. Serve with Pork Chop Gravy.

PORK CHOP GRAVY

Using the pan that the pork chops were fried in, leave a small amount of the fat and the brown crumbs. Add 3 tablespoons flour, stirring to mix with the oil and crumbs left behind. Slowly pour in 1 $\frac{1}{2}$ cups milk. Stir and cook over medium heat until it boils and is thickened. Salt and pepper to taste.

COUNTRY FRIED PORK CHOPS

This is a great cold weather dish.

4 pork chops
1 cup sliced mushrooms
1 can cream of mushroom soup
$\frac{1}{2}$-1 cup water
$\frac{1}{4}$ teaspoon leaf thyme, crushed
1 large onion, cut into chunks
1 cup sliced carrots
$\frac{1}{2}$ cup chopped celery
4 potatoes, cut into chunks
dash of salt and pepper

Brown the chops. Pour off excess fat. Stir in soup and gradually add the water and thyme. Add onions, mushrooms, carrots, celery, and potatoes. Cook over low heat for 45 minutes or until tender. Stir occasionally. Makes 4 servings.

The Earth is full of the Goodness of the Lord.

Basil   Dill   Oregano

side Dishes

You can't have a great meal
without some really good side dishes.
Here are our favorites.

SKILLET CABBAGE

Harvest time, a great time to fix this delicious vegetable combination.

- 2-3 bacon slices, cut up
- ½ head of cabbage, chopped
- 1 green pepper, chopped
- 2 stalks celery, chopped
- 3-4 tomatoes, cut up
- 1 large onion, chopped
- ⅓ cup brown sugar (or to taste)
- salt to taste

In a large skillet cook the bacon pieces, then add all the vegetables and cook on medium high stirring a few minutes. Add the brown sugar and salt, stir. Lower heat and cook 20 minutes or until vegetables are tender. Stir occasionally.

GRANDMA'S TURNIPS

A lot of people don't know what to do with turnips. Grandma Spivey is known for her turnips, and we look forward to them at our family gatherings.

- 2 pounds medium size turnips
- ½ stick butter
- ½ cup sugar
- salt and pepper

Peel turnips and chop up into ¼-inch squares. Grandma hand chops the turnips, but I use a food processor to do this. Be careful you don't overprocess them. Place turnips in a pan with ¼-½ inch of water. Add butter, and sugar to taste. Some turnips are more bitter and require more sweetening. Salt and pepper to taste. Don't shy away from the pepper, it's an important ingredient. Bring to a boil, cover and simmer 5 minutes or just until tender. It's easy to over-cook them; they should be tender but not mushy.

GRANDMA'S COOKED APPLES

Peel, core, and slice 3 pounds of apples. Use a tart apple, like a Jonathan. Put 2-3 tablespoons butter in a skillet, add the sliced apples, ½-¾ cup sugar and 1-2 teaspoons cinnamon. Cook, uncovered, stirring and turning the apples until they are tender but not mushy.

Try brown sugar instead of white sugar for a different flavor.

Where your treasure is, there your heart will be also.

Matthew 6:21

MOM'S SWEET POTATOES

A holiday tradition.

Heat in a pan 1 large can yams, then drain juice. Beat smooth with a mixer, then add:
  ½ cup sugar
  ½ stick butter melted
  2 tablespoons brown sugar
  cinnamon to taste

Mix all together and put into a 9 x 13 pan. Sprinkle mini-marshmallows on top. Bake at 400 degrees until light brown. THIS DOES NOT TAKE LONG, so watch closely.

BAKED ACORN SQUASH

Cut the acorn squash in half and remove the seeds and stringy stuff. Bake open-side down on a cookie sheet for about an hour. When the squash is tender, turn cut side up, add a pat or two of butter in the well along with 2 tablespoons of brown sugar. Sprinkle generously with cinnamon. Place back into oven and bake a few more minutes until butter melts.

BAKED RICE AND BROCCOLI

  1 ½ cups chicken broth
  ½ cup uncooked rice
  ¼ teaspoon Italian seasoning
  ¼ teaspoon garlic powder
  1 ½ cups fresh or frozen
    broccoli

Combine hot broth, rice, and seasonings. Baked covered at 375 degrees for 10 minutes. Add broccoli and bake another 20-25 minutes, covered.

Welcome ♥ Friends

MARINATED TOMATOES

This is very simple to make, a great summer addition to any meal.

Using cherry tomatoes, cut in half or use large tomatoes cut into bite-size pieces. Place tomatoes in serving bowl. Add chopped sweet onion and green pepper to taste. Stir in a generous amount of Italian salad dressing (oil and vinegar type). Allow to marinate 10 minutes before serving.

GRILLED VEGETABLES

We have an old beat-up pan that we use on the grill.

In an old baking pan, add:
  - 1-2 tablespoons olive oil, to coat bottom
  - 1 medium zucchini, sliced
  - 1 medium yellow squash, sliced
  - 1-2 medium onions, quartered
  - 1 cup of broccoli pieces
  - 1 red pepper, cut into 1-inch pieces
  - 4-5 pats of butter on top of vegetables
  - salt to taste

Cook on a grill, stirring occasionally until vegetables are tender, about 15 minutes.

GRILLED TOMATOES

When the garden is at its peak and you have too many tomatoes, try this one.

Use an old baking pan. Cut medium sized tomatoes in half and place open side up in the pan. Sprinkle with salt and garlic. Generously cover tomatoes with grated mozzarella cheese. Cook on an outdoor grill until tomatoes are tender, or grill under an oven broiler until tender and cheese is lightly toasted, approx. 10 minutes.

BROCCOLI CASSEROLE

This is a holiday favorite, perfect to take to a gathering.

    4 cups fresh broccoli pieces
    ½ package seasoned bread
        stuffing mix
    butter for stuffing mix
    2 cups mushrooms, sliced
    1 can mushroom soup
    milk

Cook broccoli until tender but crisp. Set aside and prepare according to package directions: ½ package seasoned bread stuffing. Set aside. In a saucepan heat 1 can of mushroom soup with just enough milk to make it smooth but thick. Add 2 cups fresh sliced mushrooms. Simmer until the mushrooms are cooked, about 5 minutes.

Make multiple layers in a casserole bowl, using the cooked broccoli, the prepared stuffing, the mushroom soup mixture, and mushrooms, ending with the soup on top. Heat in the microwave for 5 minutes or until very hot.

SUZY'S BAKED CORN CASSEROLE

This is a hit at our family gatherings. Better make a double recipe.

    ½ cup butter, melted
    1 small box corn muffin mix
    1 can (15 oz.) cream style corn
    1 can (15 oz.) whole kernel
        corn, drained
    1 cup sour cream

Stir all ingredients together until well blended and pour into a greased 8 x 8 baking dish. Bake at 350 degrees for 1 hour or until golden brown.

QUICK AND EASY RICE PILAF

    1 cup dry uncooked rice
    ½ stick butter
    1 package dry chicken
        noodle soup

In a saucepan melt the butter. Take the noodles and crunch them in your hands. Brown them with the butter. Add rice and 2 cups water with the soup seasoning. Bring to a boil, then cover. Reduce heat to low. Simmer for 15-20 minutes or until rice is tender.

The Lord...blesses the home of the righteous.

Proverbs 3:33

Desserts

Aren't we all watching our waistlines?
Fresh fruit
can make a nice dessert,
but occassionally something sweeter
is real nice to have... these recipes
are for those times.
We hope you enjoy some of our favorites

APPLE PIZZA DESSERT

½ loaf frozen bread dough,
  completely thawed
8 oz. cream cheese, softened
¼ cup sugar
1 egg
1 teaspoon vanilla
4 cups thinly sliced,
  peeled apples
⅔ cup sugar
¼ cup flour
1 teaspoon cinnamon

Topping:
  ⅓ cup flour
  ⅓ cup packed brown sugar
  2 tablespoons softened butter

Stretch and flatten bread dough on a greased pizza pan to the edges. Let rest for 15 minutes. Combine cream cheese, ¼ cup sugar, egg, and vanilla. Beat until smooth, spread on crust. Combine apple, ⅔ cup sugar, flour, and cinnamon, then spread on cream cheese. Combine topping ingredients until crumbly. Put them on the top. Bake at 350 degrees for 40 minutes.

APPLE CRISP

1 cup sifted flour
1 cup sugar
1 teaspoon baking powder
1 egg, well beaten
4 large apples, peeled, sliced
⅓ cup melted butter
1-2 teaspoons cinnamon

Preheat oven to 400 degrees. Put first 3 ingredients into a bowl, stirring to mix. Add egg, mix lightly with a fork until mixture is crumbly. Arrange apple slices in a greased 8-inch square pan. Top with crumbs, pour butter evenly over all, sprinkle with cinnamon. Bake at 400 degrees for 40 minutes. Serve warm.

APPLE DANISH PASTRY

This is always a special treat and is served on special occasions. Our brother brought the recipe home from Germany after he was stationed there 25 years ago.

Pastry crust:
 2 ½ cups flour
 1 teaspoon salt
 1 cup shortening
 1 egg yolk
 milk
 1 cup corn flakes

Combine flour and salt, cut in shortening. Beat the egg yolk in a measuring cup and add enough milk to make a total of ⅔ cup. Mix well. Stir into flour mixture, blending well. Knead in a little flour until not sticky. Roll out ½ of the dough into a very thin rectangle shape, fitting it into a 15 x 10 x 1 cookie sheet. After pastry is in place, sprinkle corn flakes evenly across the bottom.

Apple filling:
 8 cups of apples, peeled and
  cut in small slices
 1 cup sugar
 1-2 teaspoons cinnamon
 1 egg white

Prepare apples and stir in the sugar and cinnamon. Pour out evenly across the bottom pastry dough, over the corn flakes. Roll the second half of the pastry dough out to fit on top of apples. Seal edges and cut slits in the dough. Brush with beaten egg white. Bake 50 minutes at 375 degrees until golden brown. After baking, and while still hot, drizzle on an icing of:
 1 cup powdered sugar
 3-4 teaspoons milk
 ½ teaspoon vanilla

APPLE DUMPLINGS

6 medium size tart apples,
  peeled and cored but left whole

Mix together in a saucepan and
bring to a boil:
  1 ½ cups sugar
  1 ½ cups water
  1 teaspoon cinnamon
  3 tablespoons butter

Set aside.

For dumpling dough,
blend together:
  2 cups flour
  2 teaspoons baking powder
  1 teaspoon salt
  ⅔ cup shortening

Stir ½ cup milk into the dry
ingredients, and turn out on a
floured surface. Knead lightly,
then roll out making six, 6-inch
squares. Place an apple in the
center of the dough. Sprinkle
generously with sugar, cinnamon,
and a pat of butter. Bring corners
together at the top and pinch
closed. Place 1 inch apart in a
9 x 13 baking dish. Pour syrup
over the dumplings. Bake at 375
degrees for 35 minutes or until
apples are tender. Serve warm.

APPLE CAKE

Mix in a large bowl, blending well:
  1 cup vegetable oil
  2 cups sugar
  3 eggs, beaten
  1 teaspoon vanilla
  2 teaspoons cinnamon
  1 teaspoon nutmeg

Then stir in:
  2 cups self-rising flour
  3 cups apples, peeled
    and chopped
  1 cup pecans, chopped

Stir well, then turn into a greased
and floured cake pan. Bake at
350 degrees for 40-45 minutes
until golden brown.

The fruit of the Spirit is love, joy, peace, patience, kindness, goodness, faithfulness, gentleness and self-control.

Galatians 5:22-23

CHERRY COBBLER/ APPLE COBBLER

This is a quick dessert, sure to please any sweet tooth.

Blend together: 2 1-pound cans of cherry or apple pie filling and 2 teaspoons lemon juice. Place in a 9 x 13 baking pan. Sprinkle Crumb Top over fruit filling.

Crumb Top
Mix together until well blended and crumbly:
    1 ½ cups flour
    ¾ cup sugar
    ½ cup butter
    1-2 teaspoons cinnamon

Then add ½ cup chopped walnuts.

Bake at 400 degrees for 20-25 minutes or until top is golden brown and bubbly. Serve with a scoop of ice cream.

FRESH STRAWBERRY PIE

This pie is fragile and should be eaten the day it is fixed. It's so delicious, it's not hard to finish up. It's fast and easy to make, especially if you use a prepared pie crust.

1 prepared, baked pie crust
small pkg. strawberry gelatin

In a saucepan mix:
    1 cup cold water
    1 cup sugar
    3 heaping tablespoons
     corn starch

Bring to a boil and cook until thickened. Remove from heat and immediately sprinkle in enough strawberry gelatin to make it deep red. Set aside to cool.

Wash enough perfect strawberries to fill a pie. Remove the stems but leave the berries whole. Pour cooled (but not cold) thickened strawberry gelatin over the strawberries, stirring gently to coat all the berries. Place in the crust. Refrigerate until set. Serve with fresh whipped cream.

OUR FAVORITE PUMPKIN PIE

I have fond memories of Grandpa Spivey enjoying my pie.
He loved the molasses in it.

2 unbaked pie crusts

Mix together:
    large can of pumpkin
    1 ½ cups firmly packed
      brown sugar
    4 eggs, well beaten
    3 tablespoons melted butter
    2 tablespoons dark molasses
    1-1 ½ tablespoons pumpkin
      pie spice
    1 ¼ teaspoons salt
    1 can (1 ¼ cup) evaporated
      milk

Pour into the unbaked pie crusts and bake at 450 degrees for 10 minutes. Then reduce heat quickly by leaving oven door open a few minutes. Bake at 325 degrees for 50-55 minutes, or until a knife inserted in the middle of the pie comes out clean. Serve with whipped cream.

The earth is full of the goodness of the Lord.
Psalm 33:5

PUMPKIN ROLL

Another holiday favorite, we always make sure someone is making it for our big event.

3 eggs
1 cup sugar
⅔ cup canned pumpkin

Beat with mixer on high the eggs and sugar until fluffy, about 5 minutes. Add in pumpkin and the following dry ingredients:

1 teaspoon baking powder
1 teaspoon ginger
½ teaspoon nutmeg
½ teaspoon salt
2 teaspoons cinnamon
¾ cup flour

Mix well. Pour into a prepared 10 x 15 x 1 pan that is lined with greased and floured waxed paper. Bake 15 minutes at 350 degrees. After baking, and while still hot, turn out on a clean dish towel sprinkled with a generous amount of powdered sugar. Remove wax paper. Roll up tightly and let cool completely.

Filling:
1 cup powdered sugar
6 tablespoons butter, softened
1 8-oz. package cream cheese, softened
1 teaspoon vanilla

Beat together until creamy. Stir in ½ - 1 cup walnuts if desired. Unroll cooled pumpkin roll and spread filling evenly over entire area, re-roll, and wrap in foil. Chill, slice, and serve. Sprinkle extra powdered sugar to keep it from sticking to wrappings.

BUTTERSCOTCH PIE
For a 9 inch baked pie shell:

1 cup brown sugar packed
3 tablespoons cornstarch
2 tablespoons flour
$\frac{1}{2}$ teaspoon salt
1 cup water
1 $\frac{2}{3}$ cups milk
$\frac{1}{3}$ cup butter
3 egg yolks beaten slightly
1 $\frac{1}{2}$ teaspoons vanilla

Mix brown sugar, cornstarch, flour, and salt in a pan. Gradually stir in water and milk. Add butter. Cook over medium heat, stirring constantly until mixture thickens and boils. Boil 1 minute. Remove from heat. Gradually stir at least half of the hot mixture into egg yolks, then blend into rest of hot mixture. Boil 1 minute more, stirring constantly. Remove from heat. Blend in vanilla. Pour immediately into a baked pie shell. Cool.

CARROT CAKE
Be sure to eat your vegetables!

Blend together:
2 cups sugar
1 $\frac{1}{4}$ cups oil
2 4-oz. jars of junior carrot baby food
4 eggs
2 teaspoons cinnamon
1 $\frac{1}{2}$ teaspoons baking powder
2 cups flour

Blend all ingredients together, place in a lightly greased and floured 9 x 13 pan. Bake at 325 degrees for 45 minutes.

CREAM CHEESE FROSTING

1 8-oz. package cream cheese, softened
1 stick of butter, softened
1 teaspoon vanilla
2 cups powdered sugar.

Beat together and spread on cooled cake.

EASY CHOCOLATE BROWNIES

Who needs a mix when it's this easy?

1 stick butter
1 cup sugar
1 teaspoon vanilla
4 eggs
1 cup flour
1 can (16 oz.) chocolate syrup
½ cup chopped nuts (optional)

Mix together and pour into a greased and floured 9 x 13 pan. Bake at 350 degrees for 30 minutes. Cut into squares when cool.

PEANUT BUTTER FUDGE CAKE

Rich and creamy, everyone loves this one, especially our guys.

1 cup butter
¼ cup cocoa
1 cup water
½ cup buttermilk
2 eggs, well beaten
2 cups sugar
2 cups flour
1 teaspoon baking soda
1 teaspoon vanilla

Combine butter, cocoa, water, buttermilk, and eggs in a saucepan. Stir constantly over low heat until mixture boils. In a large bowl mix sugar, flour, and baking soda. Stir hot mixture into dry ingredients. Beat until smooth, stir in vanilla, and spread into a greased and floured 9 x 13 pan. Bake at 350 degrees for 25 minutes.

TOPPING:
1 ½ cups creamy peanut butter
1 ½ tablespoons peanut oil

Mix peanut butter and oil until smooth. Spread over cake in pan.

FROSTING:
½ cup butter
¼ cup cocoa
6 tablespoons buttermilk
4 cups confectioners' sugar
1 teaspoon vanilla

In a saucepan heat butter, cocoa, and buttermilk until bubbly. Place confectioners' sugar in bowl and beat in hot mixture. Beat until smooth, then stir in vanilla. Spread evenly over peanut butter topping. Cut into squares and serve.

CHOCOLATE CHIP GOLDEN BROWNIES

Preheat oven to 350 degrees.

    2 cups flour
    2 teaspoons baking powder
    1 teaspoon salt
    I cup butter
    I cup sugar
    I cup packed brown sugar
    1 teaspoon vanilla
    3 eggs
    12-oz. pkg. chocolate chips

Cream butter, sugar, brown sugar, and vanilla. Add baking powder, salt, and one egg at a time, mixing thoroughly. Gradually add flour, mix well. Stir in the chocolate chips.

Spread into a 15 x 10 baking pan. Bake at 350 for 30-35 minutes. Cool, cut into squares.

COOKIES AND CREAM ICE CREAM

This easy dessert is great for a home picnic.

    ½ gallon slightly soft
       vanilla ice cream
    14-oz package of chocolate
       cookies with creme centers
    ¼ cup butter
    fudge topping

Crunch up the cookies into crumbs. Set aside ⅓ cup of crumbs. Blend into the remaining crumbs ¼ cup melted butter. Press into a 9 x 13 cake pan.

Open all sides of the ice cream package. Using a large knife, slice 1½ inch thick slices of ice cream and lay on top of the crumb crust until evenly distributed. Smooth over with a spoon. Drizzle the fudge topping on top and sprinkle the ⅓ cup of reserved crumbs on top. Place in freezer several hours or overnight before serving.

I have used vanilla creme cookies for this recipe instead of the chocolate, and a caramel topping instead of fudge for a delicious change.

Cookies and Candy

Around our house cookies and holidays
go hand in hand. We love variety, and so
this collection includes our very favorites.
Most recipes have been in the family
for several generations.

NEA'S SCOTTISH SHORTBREAD

This shortbread recipe has been a family favorite for many years and was originally brought to this country by Grandma Nea from Scotland. This recipe gets better as it ages, and seems to keep forever. That is, if it's not all eaten first.

1 pound real butter
1 ⅓ cups sugar
5 ⅓ cups flour

Mix the butter and sugar on high until fluffy. Slowly add in the flour, mixing until it is well blended. It will be crumbly. Place the mixture into a lightly greased 10 x 15 x 1 pan. Press the dough into the pan until it is smooth. Make light impressions with a fork. (I actually make my impressions with a meat cleaver). Sprinkle top with sugar (optional), then bake at 350 degrees for 20 minutes, or until lightly golden. Cut into small squares while still warm. Flavor is better after it ages a day or two.

PECAN COOKIE BALLS

Scrumptious. One of our favorite holiday cookies. These freeze well, so you can prepare them ahead of the busy holiday season. The recipe calls for pecans, but we have made them with walnuts and love them this way too. Try both ways and see which you like the best.

Cream together:
    1 cup soft butter
    ¾ cup powdered sugar
    2 teaspoons vanilla
    ¼ teaspoon salt

Then blend in:
    2 cups flour
    2 cups very finely
      chopped pecans

Shape into small balls. Place on a cookie sheet and bake at 350 degrees for 15 minutes or until golden brown on the bottom of the cookie balls. Immediately after removing from oven, gently roll in powdered sugar to coat. Cool on a rack.

SPRITZ COOKIES

Cream together:
    1 cup shortening
    ¾ cup sugar
    1 egg
    ⅛ teaspoon salt
    ¼ teaspoon baking powder
    1 teaspoon almond extract

Add and blend well:
    2 cups flour

Put dough into a cookie press and make shapes. Place cookies on an ungreased cookie sheet. Sprinkle with colored sugars. Adding a piece of candied cherry to center is a delicious option. Bake at 375 degrees for 10-12 minutes, or until a light golden color.

OLD-FASHIONED CUT-OUT SUGAR COOKIES

This recipe was our mother's. We have fond memories of helping her make these, rolling out the dough and cutting out different shapes.

Cream together:
    1 cup shortening or soft butter
    2 cups sugar
    2 eggs
    2 teaspoons vanilla
    2 teaspoons baking soda
    1 teaspoon salt

Make a sour milk mixture using 2-3 tablespoons vinegar and enough milk to make 1 cup. Allow this to sit a few minutes to thicken. Blend into the shortening mixture 6 ½ cups flour, alternating flour and the milk mixture until it is well blended.

Roll the dough out onto a floured surface and knead lightly, adding in additional flour until dough is not sticky. Roll out and cut with cookie cutters. Sprinkle with sugar or if icing, don't sugar, and bake at 425 degrees for 8-10 minutes, or until light brown.

These cookies are delicious sprinkled with sugar but are also fabulous iced. If icing, let the cookies air dry for a few hours, then the cookies can be stacked and put into a container.

BASIC BUTTER ICING

    ½ cup solid vegetable
        shortening
    ½ cup soft butter
    1 teaspoon vanilla
    6 cups powdered sugar
    approx. ¼ cup milk
    dash of salt

Cream the butter, shortening, vanilla, and salt together, then add the powdered sugar. Add the milk very slowly until you achieve the desired icing consistency. Continue beating until icing is creamy smooth.

Bless the LORD,...Bless His holy name!...
Who crowns you with lovingkindness
and tender mercies,
Who satisfies your mouth with good things,
So that your youth is renewed like the eagle's.
Psalm 103

Bless His Home

Rosemary

Blessing by J.Lemming

88

GLORIOUS OATMEAL COOKIES

These are the BEST oatmeal cookies, chewy and delicious.

Cream together:
    1 cup butter, softened
    1 cup brown sugar
    1 cup white sugar

Add and beat well:
    2 eggs
    1 teaspoon vanilla
    1 teaspoon salt
    1 teaspoon baking powder

Add and thoroughly mix:
    1 ½ cups flour
    3 cups quick oatmeal

Chill about an hour. Drop spoonfuls on an ungreased cookie sheet and bake 8-10 minutes at 350 degrees.

MOLASSES COOKIES

Cream together:
    1 cup sugar
    ¾ cup shortening
    1 egg
    ¼ cup molasses

Then add:
    2 teaspoons baking soda
    ½ teaspoon salt
    1 teaspoon cinnamon
    ½ teaspoon cloves
    ½ teaspoon ginger

Blend in:
    2 cups flour

Form into cookie balls and roll in sugar. Bake at 375 degrees on an ungreased cookie sheet for 8-10 minutes. Secret: Slightly underbake...it makes them nice and chewy.

LEMON CHEESE BARS

*Light and delicious,
the ladies love this one.*

1 yellow cake with pudding mix
8 oz. cream cheese
⅓ cup sugar
1 tablespoon lemon juice
2 eggs, used separately
⅓ cup oil

Combine the dry cake mix, 1 egg, and the oil until crumbly. Reserve 1 cup of the crumbs. Place the remaining crumbs in an ungreased 9 x 13 x 2 baking pan. Bake 15 minutes at 350 degrees.

Beat cream cheese, sugar, lemon juice, and 1 egg until light and smooth. Spread over the baked layer. Sprinkle the reserved crumb mixture on top. Bake 15 minutes longer. Cut into bars after it is cool.

LUSCIOUS SUGAR COOKIES

A delicate, light cookie.

Cream together:
    1 cup sugar
    1 cup powdered sugar
    1 cup real butter
    1 cup liquid vegetable oil

Then add:
    1 teaspoon salt
    1 teaspoon baking soda
    1 teaspoon cream of tartar
    1 teaspoon vanilla

Add 4 cups of flour, mixing well. Form into balls the size of a walnut, roll in sugar, and place on an ungreased cookie sheet. Flatten with a glass. Bake at 350 degrees for 8-10 minutes or until light brown. Allow to cool slightly before removing from cookie sheet.

PRALINE GRAHAMS

These melt in your mouth. You won't believe these are made from graham crackers.

40 split (10 large)
  graham crackers
2 sticks butter
½ cup sugar
1 teaspoon vanilla
1 cup chopped pecans

Place split crackers on a 15 x 10 x 1 cookie sheet lined with foil and greased. Boil butter and sugar together 2 minutes. Remove from heat, add vanilla and pecans, and spread over crackers. Bake at 350 degrees for 10 minutes. Remove from cookie sheet promptly to cool on a rack.

SPICY GINGER CREAMS

These yummy cookies are so good, it's impossible to eat just one.

½ cup sugar
⅓ cup shortening
1 egg
½ cup molasses
½ cup water
1 teaspoon ground ginger
½ teaspoon each salt, baking soda, ground nutmeg, ground cloves, ground cinnamon
2 cups flour

Mix all ingredients together. Cover and refrigerate one hour. Drop by rounded spoonfuls onto an ungreased cookie sheet. Bake at 400 degrees for 8 minutes or until no indentation remains when touched. Remove from cookie sheet immediately. When cool, ice with Vanilla Butter Frosting.

VANILLA BUTTER FROSTING

Mix ¼ cup soft butter and 2 cups powdered sugar. Beat in 1 tablespoon milk and 1 teaspoon vanilla until smooth. Ice cookies, allowing to air dry before

OLD-FASHIONED GINGERBREAD MEN

Cream together:
   ½ cup butter
   1 cup brown sugar
   1 cup dark molasses
   2 teaspoons baking soda
   ½ teaspoon ground cloves
   1 teaspoon ground cinnamon
   2 teaspoons ground ginger
   1 teaspoon salt
   ½ cup water

Blend in 7 cups flour until well mixed. Turn out onto a lightly floured surface, roll out and cut out with gingerbread men cookie cutters. Bake at 350 degrees for 8 minutes or until cookies bounce back when touched.

Decorate with:
BASIC BUTTER ICING

   ¼ cup solid vegetable
     shortening
   ¼ cup soft butter
   ½ teaspoon vanilla
   3 cups powdered sugar
   milk (approx. ⅛ cup)
   dash of salt

Cream the butter, shortening, vanilla, and salt together, then add the powdered sugar. Add the milk very slowly until you achieve the desired icing consistency. Continue beating until icing is creamy smooth.

EASY GINGERBREAD HOUSE

Basic Butter Icing
graham crackers
fancy candies
cardboard boxes
sturdy piece of cardboard
 for base
powdered sugar

Have you ever wanted to make a gingerbread house but were afraid to make something so complicated? I have made this a number of times with kids and they love it. It's easy to succeed at this one. We once made the school my sons went to. You start with a cardboard box the size and shape you want your house to be. Place the box on a sturdy piece of cardboard as the base. I think it's fun to have a big base so there is a yard to decorate. Securely attach the building to the base with tape.

Prepare a batch of Basic Butter Icing. Using an icing decorator bag, use the icing as glue. Glue graham crackers to the box to completely cover it. After box is completely covered, glue on fancy candies to decorate it.

Use icing to fill in the cracks. Pointed ice cream cones can be covered with green icing to look like pine trees. You can make a candy stepping stone walk. Find interesting candy, and use your imagination. After all the building and decorating is completed, make it snow. Put a small amount of powdered sugar in a strainer and shake over your creation. The "snow" covers a lot of imperfections and even the youngest child can create a masterpiece to be proud of.

Decorate with:
BASIC BUTTER ICING

$\frac{1}{4}$ cup solid vegetable
 shortening
$\frac{1}{4}$ cup soft butter
$\frac{1}{2}$ teaspoon vanilla
3 cups powdered sugar
approx. $\frac{1}{8}$ cup milk
dash of salt

Cream the butter, shortening vanilla, and salt together, then add the powdered sugar. Add the milk very slowly until you achieve the desired icing consistency. Continue beating until icing is creamy smooth.

PEANUT BUTTER CHEWY CHOCOLATE COOKIES

1 ¼ cups butter, softened
2 cups sugar
2 eggs
2 teaspoons vanilla
2 cups flour
¾ cup powdered,
   unsweetened cocoa
1 teaspoon baking soda
½ teaspoon salt
2 cups (12 oz.) peanut
   butter chips

Cream butter and sugar together until light and fluffy. Add eggs and vanilla and beat well. Add cocoa, baking soda, and salt, then add flour into mixture and blend well. Stir in chips. Drop onto ungreased cookie sheet. Bake at 350 degrees for 8-9 minutes (DO NOT OVERBAKE). Cookies will be soft. They will puff while baking then flatten while cooling. Cool slightly on cookie sheet, then remove to cooling rack. Makes 4 ½ dozen.

BUCKEYES

A favorite candy, here in Ohio...
but they taste good anywhere!

1 18-oz. jar of peanut butter
1 pound powdered sugar
1 stick of butter, melted
1 teaspoon vanilla
8 oz. chocolate chips
1 tablespoon or less candy
   wax or paraffin

Mix together the peanut butter, powdered sugar, butter, and vanilla. Work with it with your hands. It will be somewhat crumbly. Form into small smooth balls. Melt the chocolate chips and a tablespoon or less of the paraffin. Dip the peanut butter balls in the chocolate, leaving a top area the size of a nickel uncovered, to resemble buckeyes. Use a toothpick to dip the balls. Allow the chocolate to set up. Store in a cool area.

PEANUT BUTTER FUDGE

This has an unusual ingredient, cheese. This no-fail fudge is delicious.

½ pound butter
½ pound Velveeta cheese
16-oz. jar of peanut butter
2 ½ pounds powdered sugar

Over low heat melt the butter. Add the Velveeta cheese and stir until melted. Now add the jar of peanut butter, stirring until it is well blended. Slowly add in the powdered sugar. As it gets thicker, you will need to knead in the remaining sugar. Press this crumbly mixture onto a 10 x 15 x 1 cookie sheet. Press and smooth out the top. Refrigerate for 30 minutes before cutting into squares. Store in the refrigerator.

EASY MICROWAVE PEANUT BRITTLE

This is so delicious and easy. It tastes every bit as good as expensive store bought.

Prepare a lightly greased cookie sheet with sides.

1 cup sugar
½ cup corn syrup
1 cup roasted, salted peanuts
1 teaspoon butter
1 teaspoon vanilla
1 teaspoon baking soda

In a 1 ½ quart casserole bowl stir together the sugar and corn syrup. Microwave on high for 4 minutes. Then stir in the peanuts. Microwave on high another 3-5 minutes or until it turns a light brown. Add the butter and vanilla and blend well. Microwave again on high for 1-2 more minutes. Peanuts will be lightly browned and the syrup very hot.

Sprinkle in the 1 teaspoon baking soda and stir gently until it is light and foamy. Quickly pour onto the lightly greased cookie sheet. Break into pieces when cool.

BUTTER TOFFEE CANDY

This is a delicious, easy candy but you must use a candy thermometer to get it to turn out right.

In a saucepan melt 1 cup real butter, then add 1 cup sugar.

Cook on high heat stirring continuously until the mixture reaches exactly 310 degrees. If it is under 310, it won't set up right. If it is over, it will burn. Use a candy thermometer.

After it reaches 310 degrees pour it onto a cookie sheet with sides. Allow to completely cool, then break into bite-size pieces.

If you desire, you can pour melted milk chocolate on top while it is still hot on the cookie sheet. If the weather is humid, I have dusted the pieces lightly with powdered sugar so they won't stick together.